START-UP
RELIGION

VISITING A CHURCH

Ruth Nason

Evans

Published by Evans Brothers Limited
2A Portman Mansions
Chiltern Street
London W1U 6NR

Reprinted 2006

Produced for Evans Brothers Limited by
White-Thomson Publishing Ltd,
Bridgewater Business Centre,
210 High Street,
Lewes, East Sussex BN7 2NH

Printed in China by WKT Co. Ltd.

Consultants: Jean Mead, Senior Lecturer in Religious
Education, School of Education, University of
Hertfordshire; Dr Anne Punter, Partnership Tutor,
School of Education, University of Hertfordshire.
Designer: Carole Binding

Cover: All photographs by Chris Fairclough

British Library Cataloguing in Publication Data
Nason, Ruth
    Visiting a church. - (Start-up religion)
    1. Public worship - Juvenile literature
    2. Church buildings - Juvenile literature
    I. Title
    264

ISBN 0 237 527677
13-digit ISBN (from 1 Jan 2007) 978 0 237 52767 9

Acknowledgements:
Special thanks to the following for their help and
involvement in the preparation of this book: Revd Peter
Barber, Revd Sarah Lowe, Revd John Fellows and all the
congregation at High Street Methodist Church,
Harpenden; the staff and children at High Beeches
Primary School.

Picture Acknowledgements:
John Barringer: page 15 bottom left; Chris Fairclough
Colour Library: pages 4 top left, 4 top right, 4 centre,
4 bottom centre; Michael Nason: pages 13 top right,
13 centre, 13 bottom left, 15 top left.
All other photographs by Chris Fairclough.

Contents

Church buildings

Which of these buildings is a church? How can you tell?

There are many types of churches. The pictures in this book show the inside of this Methodist church.

church   Methodist

On a map, churches are marked with a cross.
How many churches are on this map?

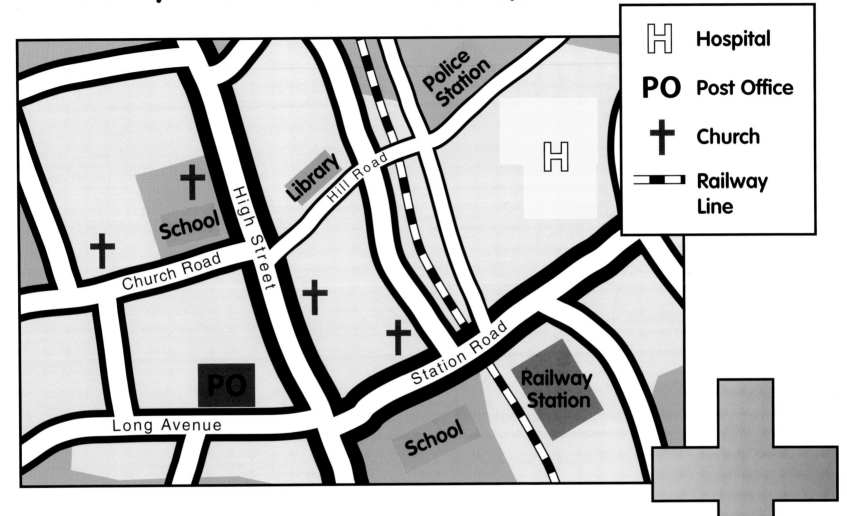

A cross is a symbol of Christianity. Can you think
of places where you see a cross symbol like this?
Look for crosses in the pictures in this book.

cross   symbol   Christianity

Inside a church

► On Sundays, many Christians go to a service at church.

A minister talks to the people. This church has three ministers.

The people at the service are called the congregation.

Christians   service   minister

Some churches have a choir.

▼ At the service, people think about God. They sing hymns, which tell God how they feel.

congregation   choir   God   hymns   **7**

A special place

A church is a special place for Christians. They go there to worship God, to pray and to learn about Jesus.

They believe that Jesus is God's son, who taught people about God's love.

Can you see the picture of the baby Jesus in this stained-glass window?

special   worship   pray   Jesus

◀ **The church is a quiet place to think and pray.**

▼ **What are these people doing to help make their church a special place?**

believe   stained-glass   quiet   9

A school visit

When you visit a church with your school, it will probably be empty.

How do you think the people who worship there would like you to behave?

behave

▲ **These visitors thought the church was:**

beautiful big quiet pretty peaceful

They noticed details like these:

Which can you find in the big picture?

Parts of a church

The children saw that the church floor was in the shape of a cross.

Organ

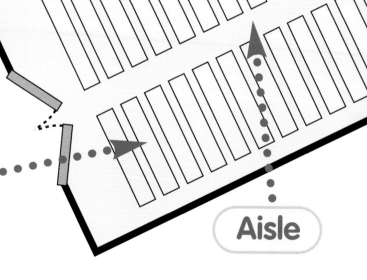

Aisle

▲ The minister asked if they could put names on parts of the church.

Pews

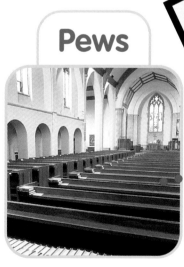

organ pews aisle pulpit

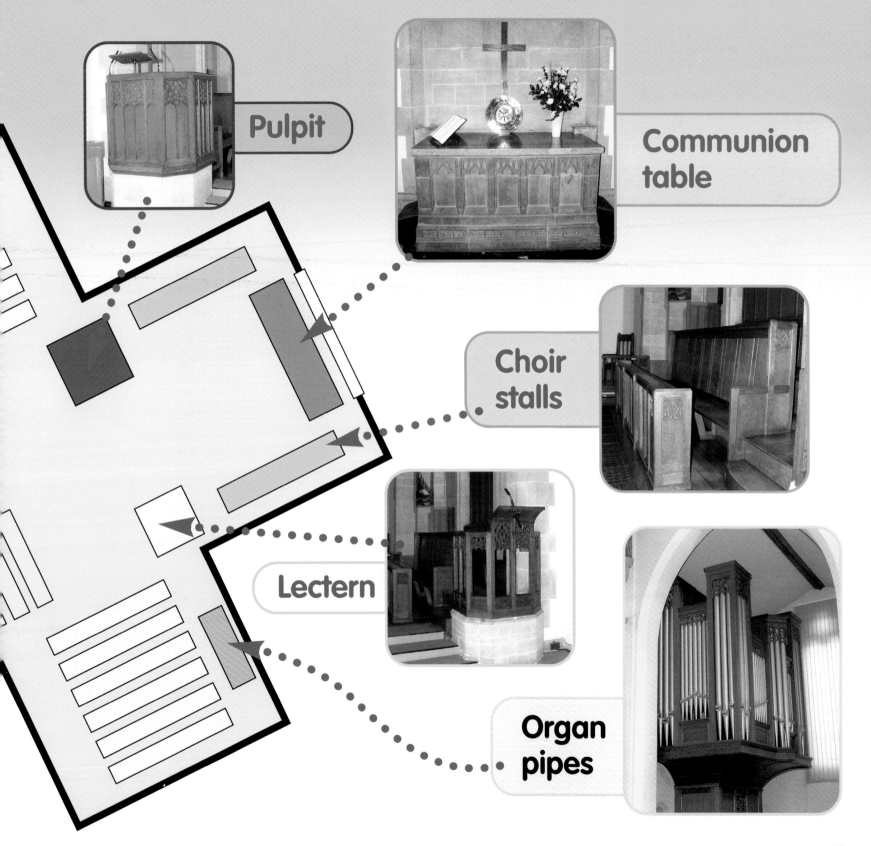

Pulpit

Communion table

Choir stalls

Lectern

Organ pipes

communion table   choir stalls   lectern   13

Pulpit, lectern and font

◀ In a service, the minister goes into the pulpit to talk to the people. This talk is called the sermon.

▶ Why do you think the pulpit is built higher than the church floor?

sermon   Bible

► A lectern is a reading desk. In a service, someone stands at the lectern to read out part of the Bible. The Bible is the holy book with stories about God and Jesus.

◄ The font is used for a baptism. The minister splashes water on the baby's head.

holy book   font   baptism   **15**

Music in church

Many people enjoy singing in church.

▶ When you visit a church, look for hymn books.••••▶ 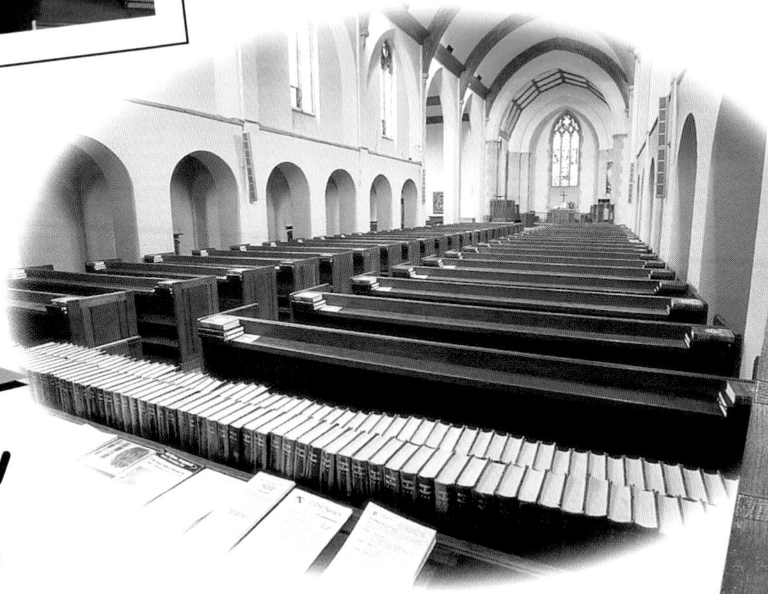 Hymn boards show the numbers of the hymns that the people will sing.

HYMNS
28
806
1
36

▼ In many churches an organist plays the music for the hymns. He uses his hands on the organ keys and his feet on the pedals.

► The sound comes from the organ pipes.

organist   keys   pedals

The communion table

▶ The communion table is at the front of the church.

▼ At communion services, the table is set with bread and wine.

Many Christians have services where they share bread and wine. Jesus told his followers to do this as a way of remembering him.

communion services   share

◀ **The minister breaks the bread.**

▼ **She shares the bread and wine with the congregation.**

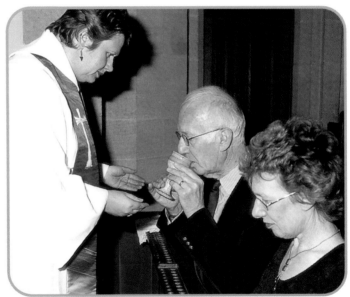

Above the communion table is a cross. Jesus died on a cross, but Christians believe that he came alive again and now he lives with God, his father.

Many rooms

The church shown in this book has many rooms.
It is open every day, for people to visit.

◀ In the office, people help to plan the ministers' work.

▶ People come to talk to the ministers.

office   Junior Church

▶ **There are rooms where the Junior Church meets on Sundays.**

▲ **There is a library and a café.**

Can you see what happens in these rooms that is welcoming to visitors?

library   café   welcoming

Further information for

New words introduced in the text:

aisle	Christianity	cross	Junior Church	organist	service
baptism	Christians	details	keys	peaceful	share
behave	church	followers	lectern	pedals	special
believe	communion	font	library	pews	stained-glass
Bible	services	God	Methodist	pray	symbol
café	communion	holy book	minister	pulpit	welcoming
choir	table	hymns	office	quiet	worship
choir stalls	congregation	Jesus	organ	sermon	

Suggested Activities

If possible, use this book in conjunction with a real visit to a local church. The local RE advisor or SACRE (Standing Advisory Council on Religious Education) may be able to provide information about churches willing to host visits. Consider using a 'virtual visit', via a website or CD rom, to supplement a visit, or if a real visit is not possible. Videos and pictures of the church in use, and interviews with members, are useful supplements to visiting an empty building. This book can help prepare for such a visit and/or be used as follow-up. The church in the book is a Methodist church. Explore in what ways another church is the same or different. Try to avoid stereotypes by using resources showing a range of cultures if possible.

PAGES 4-5
Take digital photographs of local buildings, including the school and churches. Let children identify them and sort them into sets. Link them to a local map for display.

Discuss same/different/similar.
Start a 'cross collection' of pictures and label the places where they were seen (include jewellery and 'crossed fingers').

PAGES 6-7
Show a video clip of church worship.
Ask a member of a local church to come in to school and tell what they do there and how they feel about it.
Play the finger game: 'Here's the church and here's the steeple, look inside and here are the people'. Explain that the people are the church too, not just the building where they meet (cf 'a good school' can mean the people not the building).

PAGES 8-9
Talk about the children's own 'special places', private or shared, where they go to think.
Make a class list of all jobs needed to make a place special – interview the school caretaker.

Parents and Teachers

PAGES 10-11

Talk about showing respect appropriately in different places (e.g. outdoor shoes off in gym, not jumping on grandma's sofa, not eating in shops). Prepare for suitable behaviour in church, but don't make it intimidating.

If you visit a church, make time to be quiet and become aware of the atmosphere. Children's responses to it may vary.

PAGES 12-13

Enlarge the plan of the church, or make one of the church you visit. Make cards of pictures and of names of church items – then play a 'matching pairs' game and place them on the plan.

PAGES 14-15

Ask someone from a local church to bring some items (e.g. Bible, hymn books, hassocks, cross, a crucifix) for children to draw and discuss so that they can recognize them on a visit. Find and read a Bible story the children know, and a hymn they may be familiar with (carols?).

PAGES 16-17

Listen to tapes or videos of church music of various types ('gospel' songs or songs of praise as well as organ music). Play a maths 'find the hymn number' game with a 'hymn board' if you can have access to a set of song books.

PAGES 18-19

Tell the story of Jesus' last supper (NB it is not appropriate to role-play a communion).

Discuss how food can remind us of someone or some event, using children's own experiences. Discuss (and make?) what would be a good food symbol to remind them of a class event or known person.

Recommended Resources

WEBSITES

The following RE 'gateway' sites provide helpful recommendations for videos and books and links to organisations, sources of artefacts and other useful websites for teachers and pupils.

http://www.theREsite.org.uk has 80 sites on Christianity for Key Stage 1.
http://re-xs.ucsm.ac.uk has introductory information, teachers' page, lots of links.
http://theredirectory.org.uk has links to organisations and resources.
http://www.educhurch.org.uk is an excellent site about three churches and their members.
http://www.methodist.org.uk
http://www.findachurch.co.uk

VIDEOS

BBC 'Watch' series on Places of Worship for KS1.

PAGES 20-21

If you go to a church, ask to see around various rooms. Look for clues about how the building is used by a living community, especially if it is a 'historic' building. Avoid the impression that religion is something people used to do in the olden days.

Index